W9-AUZ-101

WALLINGFORD PUBLIC LIBRARY
WALLINGFORD, CONNECTICUT 06492

PANAMA

A TRUE BOOK

by
Dana Meachen Rau

Children's Press®

A Division of Grolier Publishing

New York London Hong Kong Sydney
Danbury, Connecticut

WALLINGFORD PUBLIC LIBRARY
WALLINGFORD, CONNECTICUT 06492

J972.87
RAU

Reading Consultant
Linda Cornwell
Learning Resource Consultant
Indiana Department of
Education

A Panamanian schoolchild

Visit Children's Press® on the
Internet at:
http://publishing.grolier.com

Library of Congress Cataloging-in-Publication Data

Rau, Dana Meachen, 1971-
    Panama / by Dana Meachen Rau
        p.   cm.—(A True book)
    Includes bibliographical references and index.
    Summary: Provides an overview of the geography, history, and culture
of the small North American country that touches two oceans and links
two continents.
    ISBN: 0-516-21189-7 (lib. bdg.)   0-516-26497-4 (pbk.)
    1. Panama—Juvenile literature. [1. Panama.] I. Title. II. Series.
F1563.2.R38   1999   98-2812
972-87—dc21   21.00/12.58 5/99   CIP
                                                                      AC

GROLIER
PUBLISHING

©1999 Children's Press®,
a Division of Grolier Publishing Co., Inc.
All rights reserved. Published simultaneously in Canada.
Printed in the United States of America.
1 2 3 4 5 6 7 8 9 10 R 08 07 06 05 04 03 02 01 00 99

Contents

Crossroads of the World 5

The Land between Two Oceans 7

Visiting a Tropical Forest 12

A Changing History 16

Canal for the World 23

A Mix of People 30

Panamanian Life 36

To Find Out More 44

Important Words 46

Index 47

Meet the Author 48

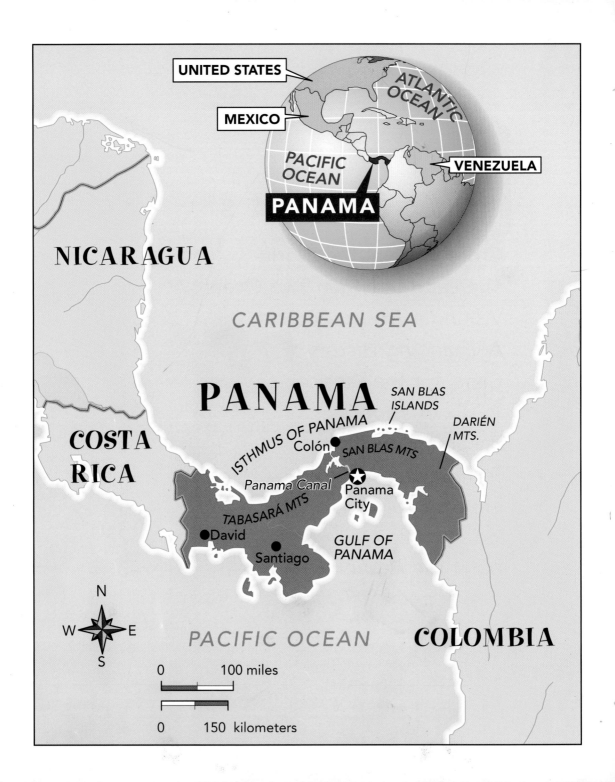

Crossroads of the World

A crossroads is a place where different things come together. Imagine how amazing it would be to live in the country called the "crossroads of the world."

Panama is an S-shaped country that touches two oceans and links two continents. It is filled with many types of animals, plants, and people. Panama is an isthmus—a narrow strip of land that connects two larger pieces of land. This tiny Central American country touches an arm of the Atlantic Ocean called the Caribbean Sea in the north and the Pacific Ocean in the south. Costa Rica lies on its western border, and Colombia is on its eastern border.

The Land between Two Oceans

If you lived in Panama, you might ride a canoe on one of its five hundred rivers, or fish on one of its eight hundred coastal islands. You might hike in the Tabasará Mountains in the west, or the San Blas or Darién Mountains in the east.

Panamanians enjoy swimming and snorkeling in the waters of the San Blas Islands.

You might work on the farm-land between the mountains and the coasts.

The Panama Canal cuts through the center of Panama

and connects the Atlantic and
Pacific oceans. Almost all of
the 2.5 million people in
Panama live near the canal or
on the Pacific coast west of

A ship prepares to enter the canal.

Few people live in the tropical rain forests of eastern Panama.

the canal. East of the canal lies the region of Darién. Darién is so thick with tropical rain forests and swamps that very few people live there.

The air in Panama almost always feels wet—even when it's not raining. The rainy season lasts from April to December. The dry season runs from January to March. Panama's temperature is warm all year round.

Visiting a Tropical Forest

Colorful orchids and cashew trees thrive in the warm, wet air of Panama's tropical rain forests. Sugarcane, mangoes, and plantains grow there, too. *Plantanos* (plantains) are a favorite fruit in Panama. They look a lot like bananas.

The national flower of Panama is a white orchid called the *Flor del Espíritu Santo* ("Flower of the Holy Spirit").

Big cats, such as pumas and jaguars, roam these forests. So do tapirs, sloths, and boars. Many kinds of monkeys swing through the trees.

A few of the creatures found in the rain forest include the sloth (top), the poison-dart frog (left), and the blue morpho butterfly (right).

High up in the rain forest trees, you can see large vultures and tiny hummingbirds. You might catch a glimpse of the beautiful blue morpho butterfly. At night, bats zip through the air.

Snakes and crocodiles, toads and frogs, spiders and scorpions, and hundreds of kinds of ants also live in the rain forest. Sharks, dolphins, lobsters, and shrimp swim in the waters off Panama's coast.

A Changing History

American Indians were the first people to use Panama as a crossroads. They came into Panama from Mexico and Peru. For hundreds of years, they fished, hunted, and farmed there.

Explorers from Spain, across the Atlantic Ocean, were inter-

Balboa called the ocean he saw on the other side of Panama the Great South Sea. It was later renamed the Pacific Ocean.

ested in the Americas. They believed they would find gold there. In 1501, Spanish explorer Rodrigo de Bastidas became the first European to reach Panama. By 1510, groups of people came to settle. Spanish explorer Vasco Núñez de Balboa was one of these settlers. In 1513, Balboa was the first European to cross Panama to see the Pacific Ocean.

The Spaniards killed many Indians and took their land. When the Spaniards conquered Peru, they found a lot of gold treasure. They built a stone road across Panama for mules to help carry the gold from Peru to their ships.

Colombia was another Spanish settlement in the

Americas. In 1819, Colombia broke away from Spain. Soon after, in 1821, Panama also broke away from Spain. It became a province of Colombia.

Tourists explore the remains of the early Spanish colonies.

Later, the people of Panama wanted to control their own country. With help from the United States, Panama became an independent nation on November 3, 1903.

In return for helping them win independence, Panama agreed to let the United States build a canal across Panama. The Panama Canal links the Atlantic and Pacific oceans.

After Panama became an independent nation, it continued

The United States builds a canal across Panama.

to have an unstable government. Then in 1983, General
Manuel Antonio Noriega took
over as head of the military and
ruled Panama. He was a dis-
honest leader who committed

many crimes. The United States helped remove Noriega from power in 1990. Guillermo Endara then became president of Panama. He was followed by President Ernesto Perez Balladares in 1994.

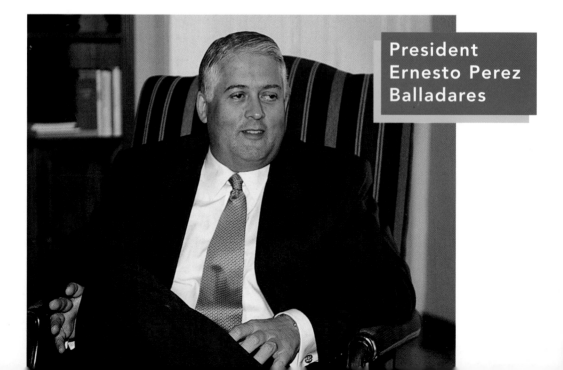

President Ernesto Perez Balladares

Canal for the World

The Panama Canal made shipping easier for countries all over the world. Before it was built, ships traveling from the Atlantic to the Pacific had to make a long trip around South America. The canal made the journey 7,000 miles (11,250 kilometers) shorter.

Tools were left behind by the French after their unsuccessful attempt to complete the canal.

In 1882, a French company was the first to try to build a canal. But workers had many problems with diseases spread by mosquitoes and mud slides. In 1904, Panama and the United States signed a treaty that gave the United States control of the Canal Zone. The Canal Zone is a strip of land 10 miles (16 km) wide across Panama where the canal would be built. In return, the United States paid Panama for use of the canal.

Workers from the United States
surveyed possible canal routes.

About 35,000 workers
came from 97 countries to
build the Panama Canal. It
took ten years, and cost

almost $400 million and many of the workers' lives. On August 15, 1914, the first ship passed through the canal.

Panama and the United States signed two more treaties in 1977. These treaties will return the Canal Zone to Panama in 2000. Today, the canal is not used as much as it was in past years. Many modern ships are too large to fit through it.

The Panama Canal

A ship enters the Gatun Locks.

The Panama Canal is a lock-and-lake canal. A lock is like a large bathtub with doors at each end. When a ship enters a lock, the doors close, and the lock fills with water until the ship floats up to the level of the next lock. Like steps, the ship moves up from lock to lock until it reaches the level of the mountains running through the center of Panama. There, it has an easy trip across Gatun Lake. Then, on the other

A ship on the Gaillard Cut channel.

side of the lake, the ship is lowered back down through locks to sea level. The canal is about 50 miles (80 km) long, and the trip takes about nine hours.

A ship leaves the canal at the Miraflores Lock.

A Mix of People

People who live in Panama today are descended from many different ethnic groups. *Mestizos* make up most of the population. They are part Spanish and part American Indian. Other people are descended from the original Spanish settlers,

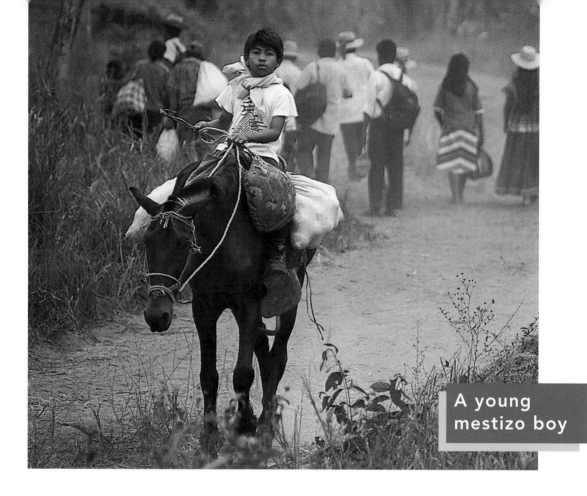

A young
mestizo boy

African slaves, or canal workers
from all around the world.

The smallest group today is
American Indian. They are
descendants of the people

The main Indian groups that live in Panama are the Chocó (left), the Cuna (below), and the Guaymí (opposite page).

who lived in Panama before the Spaniards arrived. Three groups of Indians still follow the ancient traditions of their ancestors.

The Chocó, who live in the forests of Darién, are known for building *piraguas* (canoes).

They hold a special ceremony when a new piragua is released onto the river.

The Cuna people live on Panama's northern shores and on the San Blas Islands. They grow crops and are skilled at creating decorative cloths called *molas*.

The Guaymí are the largest Indian group. They live in the northwestern areas of Panama. Music is an important part of their culture.

Making Molas

Mola-making is an important craft among the Cuna Indians. Molas are pieces of cloth decorated with thread. They take months to make. Some molas are worn every day, and some are kept for special occasions. Subjects of a mola design may be birds, flowers, animals, or people.

Above: A Cuna Indian sews a mola. Right: A completed mola featuring a bird design

Panamanian Life

People who live in Panama are called Panamanians. Many of their beliefs and customs come from Spanish traditions. Almost all Panamanians speak Spanish. Most Panamanians follow the Roman Catholic religion, which also came to Panama from Spain. Panama's

The Plaza Cathedral (above), and the statue of Balboa (right) are both located in Panama City.

money is even called the *balboa*, named after the Spanish explorer. Indian tribes still speak their own languages and practice their own religious traditions.

The government in Panama is a republic. In a republic, people elect a president. A legislature makes the laws, and a court system helps put the laws into effect.

Farming and fishing are two main industries in Panama. One out of every four people working in Panama is a farmer. Farmers grow bananas, sugar, and coffee. On the coasts, people fish for shrimp. Panama sells these items to other countries.

Many crops and fish are used by Panamanians to create delicious dishes. Rice and beans is a popular meal. People also enjoy *tortillas*, which are similar to pancakes made of cornmeal.

Many Panamanians cook rice with beans to make a dish called *guacho*.

A view of
Panama City

More than half of Panama's people live in the cities. The cities are centers for business and trade. Panama City, the capital of Panama, is the largest city.

All over Panama, education is important. Starting at age five, all children have to go to school. Nine out of ten people in Panama can read and write.

Panamanians celebrate many festivals. Once a year, businesses and schools across Panama close for Carnival time. People parade through the streets, dancing and singing. One of the most popular dances is called the

A couple dances the tamborito.

tamborito, meaning "little drum." While the dancers step and spin, people surround them, clapping their hands.

Panamanians celebrate their culture with parades, dancing, and singing.

Panama's crossroads of land, nature, and culture have given the people of Panama many reasons to celebrate.

To Find Out More

Here are some additional resources to help you learn more about the nation of Panama:

 **Books**

Chinery, Michael. **Rainforest Animals.** Random House, 1992.

Clarke, Penny. **Rainforest.** Franklin Watts, 1996.

Parker, Nancy Winslow. **Locks, Crocs, and Skeeters: The Story of the Panama Canal.** Greenwillow Books, 1996.

Petersen, David. **South America.** Children's Press, 1998.

Winkelman, Barbara Gaines. **The Panama Canal.** Children's Press, 1998.

Organizations and Online Sites

Panama Canal Commission
Unit 2300
APO AA 34011-2300
http://www.pananet.com/ pancanal

The Panama Canal Commission is a part of the U. S. government. Its website contains maps, photos, and a full history of the Panama Canal.

Rainforest Action Network
221 Pine Street, Suite 500
San Francisco, CA 94104
http://www.ran.org/

Visit the Kids' Corner at the Rainforest Action Network's website to explore the rain forest and meet the animals and people that live there. Also, find out what you can do to help save rain forests around the world.

Smithsonian Tropical Research Institute (STRI)
Visitor Services Office
Unit 0948
APO AA 34002-0948
http://www.stri.org/

The Smithsonian Tropical Research Institute, based in Panama, is one of the world's leading centers for studying tropical habitats. Visit their website to read about their latest programs and find out news about the institute.

The United Nations
New York, NY 10017
http://www.un.org/Pubs/ CyberSchoolBus

The United Nations' Cyber School Bus takes you to countries all over the world. Take quizzes, play games, look at flags, and find facts about Panama and a lot of other countries.

Important Words

continent one of the seven large land masses of Earth

descended to be related to people from the past

independent to be free from another country's control

industry a type of business or trade

isthmus a narrow strip of land that lies between two bodies of water and connects two larger land masses

province a smaller part of a bigger country

treaty an agreement between two or more countries

46

Index

(**Boldface** page numbers
   indicate illustrations.)

animals, 12–15, **14**
Atlantic Ocean, 9, 16, 20, 23
Balladares, Ernesto Perez,
   22, **22**
Canal Zone, 25, 27
Caribbean Sea, 6
Colombia, 6, 19
Darién Mountains, 7, 11, 33
de Balboa, Vasco Núñez,
   17, **18, 37**
de Bastidas, Rodrigo, 17
economy, 38–39
education, 41
Endara, Guillermo, 22
entertainment, 41–42
explorers, 16–17, 37
Gatun Lake, 28
government, 21–22, 38
Indians,
   American, 16, 18, 30, 31
   Chocó, **32,** 33
   Cuna, **32,** 34, **35**
   Guaymí, **33,** 34

isthmus, 6
mestizos, 30, **31**
molas, 34–35, **35**
Noriega, Manuel
   Antonio, 21–22
Pacific Ocean, 6, 9, 17,
   20, 23
Panama Canal, 8, 20, **21,**
   23, 25–29, **28–29**
Panama City, **9,** 40, **40**
Panamanians, 36, 39,
   41
Peru, 16, 18
piraguas (canoes), 33–34
plants, 12, **13**
rain forest, **10,** 11, 12
Roman Catholic, 36, **37**
San Blas, 7, **8,** 34
Spain, 16, 19, 36
Spaniards, 18, 33
Tabasará Mountains, 7
tamborito, 42, **42**
tortillas, 39
United States, 20, 22, 25,
   27

Meet the Author

Ever since Dana Meachen Rau can remember, she has loved to write. A graduate of Trinity College in Hartford, Connecticut, Dana works as a children's book editor and has authored many books for children, including biographies, nonfiction, early readers, and historical fiction. She has also won writing awards for her short stories.

When Dana is not writing, she is doing her favorite things—watching movies, eating pizza, and looking at the stars—with her husband, Chris, and son, Charlie, in Farmington, Connecticut.

Photographs ©: D. Donne Bryant Stock Photography: 37 left, 42 (Byron Augustin); Dave G. Houser: 32 top, 35 bottom; Envision: 39 (Steven Needham); Gamma-Liaison: 2 (Wolfgang Kaehler), 22 (Alyx Kellington); North Wind Picture Archives: 24 top, 26; Panos Pictures: 19, 31 (Jon Mitchell); Peter Arnold Inc.: 37 right (Martha Cooper), 1 (Clyde H. Smith); Photo Researchers: 14 top (Jack Fields), 14 bottom left (S. R. Maglione), 14 bottom right (Lawrence Migdale); Photri: 8, 10; South American Pictures: cover (Robert Francis), 32 bottom (Tony Morrison); Stock Montage, Inc.:18, 24 bottom; Superstock, Inc.: 21; Tony Stone Images: 9 (Will & Deni McIntyre), 35 top (Tom & Michelle Grimm), 29 (Will and Deni McIntyre), 28 (Cathlyn Melloan), 40 (Mark Segal), 13 (Art Wolfe); Viesti Collection, Inc.: 33, 43 (Joe Viesti). Map by Joe Le Monnier.

j972.87   Rau, Dana Meachen,
RAU   1971-

          Panama.

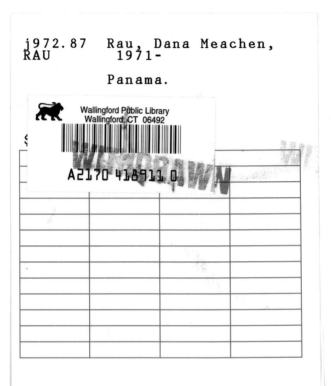

Wallingford Public Library
Wallingford, CT 06492

A2170 418911 0

WITHDRAWN

CHILDREN'S LIBRARY

WALLINGFORD PUBLIC LIBRARY
200 NO MAIN ST
WALLINGFORD CT 06492

BAKER & TAYLOR